Thank you!

My Music Book

THE POETRY OF
LARRY TOUSSAINT GARLINGTON

*Featuring the timeless songs
that inspired my pen*

PUBLISHING INFORMATION

The Garlington House
322 Meadow Street
Suite 1
Agawam, MA 01001
Phone: 1-203-565-3577

Published by The Garlington House 05/01/2016

ISBN: 978-0-692-62544-6

Library of Congress Control Number: 2016905600

Any people depicted in stock imagery provided by Thinkstock are models,
and such images are being used for illustrative purposes only.
Certain stock imagery © Thinkstock.

Due to the dynamic nature of the Internet, any web addresses or links contained in this book may have
changed since publication and may no longer be valid. The views expressed in this work are solely those of the author.

Photo Credits: The Musical Image Used on the Front and Back Covers was photographed by: Stasyuk
Stanislav/Stock Photo//photos.com

Dedication

This book is dedicated to lasting memories of my grandmother, Annie "Tooie" Ward and to the enduring spirit and presence of my mother, Laura "Pie" Garlington - still strong and feisty at age 88, and subject of the poem, "Golden Lady".

Cover Photo
by

VIRGILIO GONZALEZ

www.vrgonzalez.com

Special Acknowledgement

"When does it, where does it, and why does love go wrong?
Why does it come unglued, unhinged, unfastened, undone?"

(My Blue Epiphany)

Love can be a compelling motivator. Whether you're "in it" or "out of it", regretful or proud of it, the journals of love are deep and bountiful. I consider myself a survivor in the game of life and love. Having been married for over thirty years, I don't look upon my recent divorce as a failing. I prefer the positive, as in the "glass is half full". I only need look at my two children as confirmation. I'd do it all again because I was truly in love. And how many times does one get to say that in a lifetime? So why does love go wrong? I don't know. But I feel fortunate to have experienced its wonders and allure, to have swum in its waters and emerged wiser, with my heart intact and a sense of family that can never be taken away. I'm better for it. Thank you, Sheila. May we remain friends, live healthy lives and enjoy the "coming new", as provided by our darlings, Kia, Julian, our beautiful grandsons, Khari and Jordan, as well as our daring, surviving selves.

Acknowledgements

Many thanks to Eileen Harris of **EH Graphics** for providing beautiful and appropriate visuals throughout this book – along with the occasional edit. Thank you for reading my stuff! You have a keen sense of what works. We changed course a few times along the way, *but we made it!*

ALL GRAPHICS AND ARTWORK

CREATED OR PROVIDED BY:

EH GRAPHICS
www.ehgraphics.com

Introduction

"Music touches the innocence, my innocence. Even snow plays a tune when falling, for those who choose to listen."
(Abstract Painting)

My poetry spans many moods, but music sets it. Music inspires me – Always has. When I was a young man of seventeen, I fancied myself a singer, but each time I felt the urge to compose, the melody would slip away and I'd be left alone with lyrics. It's how I arrived. For me, poetry and music are forever intertwined. Are Stevie and Sting so different from Maya and Emily? In style and delivery, certainly, but in spirit, I think not. Writers are writers, and all are in the business of communication. Each verse, each stanza, must have a certain flow, a certain rhythm in order to be truly complete. If given chance, it'll speak to those who choose to listen. I am inspired by song! And so I've decided to showcase these two forms, music and poetry, one alongside the other, the cause and effect, as it were. I've chosen forty three songs that have served, through the years, in some form or fashion as inspiration for my musings. I invite you to take it all in and fully immerse yourself in the music and the rhyme.

"BABY I'M A STAR": Written and performed by Prince.

"Baby I'm a star. Might not know it now". Prince is a musical genius, but in many ways, he's just like the rest of us. *"We all long to hear, the wonderful sound, of applause"*.

Poem which it inspired: **APPLAUSE**

"HEAVEN IS TEN ZILLION LIGHT YEARS AWAY": Written and performed by Stevie Wonder.

"Where is your God? That's what my friends ask me. And I say: It's taking Him so long, cause we've got so far to come". Stevie is just special; His songs are so reflective. He seems to be saying here; Be patient. God is watching.

Poem which it inspired: **JOURNEY TO THE DAY**

"NOWHERE MAN": Written by Lennon - McCartney. Performed by The Beatles.

A song from my youth; I recall being struck by the lyrics − *"He's a real nowhere man, sitting in his nowhere land, making all his nowhere plans, for nobody. Isn't he a bit like you and me?"* I think we've all fallen into ruts at some point in our lives, feeling perhaps, that we were underachieving, that we could be doing more.

Poem which it inspired: **WISDOM**

"SUPER FREAK": Written by Rick James, Alonzo Miller. Performed by Rick James.

"She's a very kinky girl". Rick James was a one-of-a-kind talent. His music always had an edge and encouraged me to approach writing without a safety net. I still constrict myself from time to time, but when I think of Rick James' gifts to the world, I think − ***Go for it!***

Poem which it inspired: **DAMN! BABY!**

"SAY IT LOUD! I'M BLACK AND I'M PROUD": Written and performed by James Brown. This song made an indelible impression on me as a youngster. I recall it being an anthem of sorts for black America during the turbulent sixties. I've no doubt that it influenced my writing and my life as well. I'm proud of my race and have taught my children to be proud and accepting of others.

Poem which it inspired: **STAND**

"BEAUTIFUL BOY": Written and performed by John Lennon.
"Before you cross the street, take my hand. Life is just what happens to you, while you're busy making other plans. Beautiful, Beautiful, Beautiful, Beautiful Boy".

Poem which it inspired: **MY SON** (For Julian Toussaint)

"A CHANGE IS GONNA COME": Written and performed by Sam Cooke

A heart-wrenching song by one of soul music's masters. This song is synonymous with the Civil Rights Movement of the sixties, but its promise is needed still, today.

Poem which it inspired: **CHICAGO ON FIRE!**

Chapter 1

WELCOME MOOD

An aura of peace fills a sunlit room

Where the poet dwells and happiness looms

Where the mere presence of paper and pen

Is company enough for the writing man.

Welcome inside my pages of life

Where stories are told and feelings shared

Where an intimate spool of fact and fantasy

Spins to your delight.

EMPIRE STATE OF MIND

Words & Music by Shawn Carter, Alexander Shuckburgh, Janet Sewell-Ulepic, Alicia Keys, Angela Hunte, Sylvia Robinson & Bert Keyes

"New York"
inspired by:

EMPIRE STATE OF MIND

By: Jay-Z, Alicia Keys
Written by - Angela Hunte, Alicia
     Keys, Alexander Shuckburgh,
     Burt Keyes, Jane't "Jnay"
     Sewell-Ulepic, Shawn Carter,
     Sylvia Robinson
Album: "The Blue Print 3"
Original Release Date: October 2009
Genre: Rap/Hip Hop
Label: Rock Nation

NEW YORK

UPTOWN WALKING AND WINTER DAYS
PEOPLE DREAMS AND BROADWAY PLAYS
SPANNING THE GLOBE IN DIFFERENT FACES,
LUNCH IN FANCY PLACES.

NEW YORK SATISFIES THE RUNNING MIND
ISSUING CHARGES OF SPECTACLE AND FAME
THE TOUCH, SIGHT, SOUND OF EXCITEMENT,
BORN TO ENDURE! NEVER TO BE TAMED!

"Star Dancer"
inspired by:

Aquarius
By: The Fifth Dimension
Music by: Galt MacDermot
Lyrics – James Rado &
      Gerome Ragni
Written for: "Hair" (Broadway Play)
Original release date: 1967
Label: Bell
Genre: Pop/New Age/Broadway

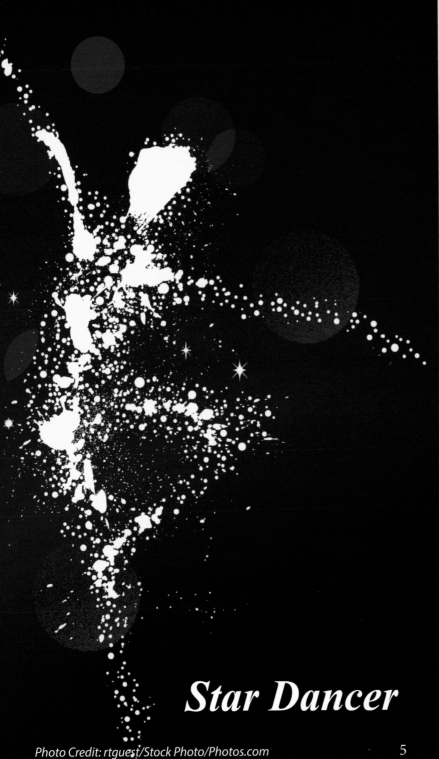

She'll not bemuse nor betray, only shine in your way

Star dancer burning, a trillion miles near

Beautifying a silent night, as many around her often do

She smiles upon a place of love

And negates all need for city light.

Star Dancer,

I have gazed above on many occasions

For romanticism lurks in your homeward space

An enthralling story you will always tell

One that satisfies, completes my day

I believe in miracles and dreams come true

Wishes that abound, and you

Star Dancer,

Forever, your signature marks an open sky

Scorching bright, color my world, Star Dancer,

Goodnight.

Star Dancer

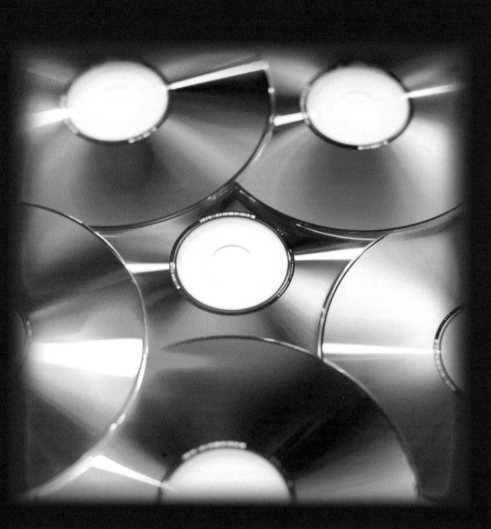

BABY I'M A STAR

Words and Music by
PRINCE

Bright Rock beat

N.C.

mf

C D   Bm D   Dsus 2

"Applause"
inspired by:

Baby I'm A Star
By: **Prince**
Written by: **Prince**
Album: **"Purple Rain"**
Original Release Date: **1984**
Label: **Warner Brothers**
Genre: **New Wave / Funk Rock**

I believe we all yearn in some child-like way
To dazzle in the spotlight at front and center stage
To one day speak from the grand podium
While listening eyes Rave and never once stray.

Applause, like an old song or cornered souvenir
The memory embeds the very moment you hear
For that duration of acceptance is our time in a bottle
We bask in the happening, then reflect tomorrow.

It is high and never low; it is found and never lost
When coming from the heart, it will surely cost
For a tear will start to glisten, you have truly been touched
A timely pat on one's back is never too much
We all long to hear the wonderful sound,
Of applause.

"I Wish"
inspired by:

Beautiful Day
By: U2
Music by: U2
Lyrics – BONO
Album: All That You Can't Leave Behind
Original Release Date: 2000
Label: Island Records, Interscope Records
Genre: Rock/Pop Rock

I WISH

A picture briefly frozen at twelve o'clock high

A sudden twist!

Beginning her descending dive

I wish to capture that instant she hides

But all to no avail, for just as I arrive

Sundown.

"Make Me Laugh"
inspired by:

I SMILE
By: **Kirk Franklin**
Written by: **Kirk Franklin,**
    James Harris, Terry Lewis,
    Fredrick Tackett
Album: **"Hello Fear"**
Original Release Date: **2011**
Genre: **Christian & Gospel**
Label: **2011 Verity Gospel Music**
    Group

Make Me Laugh . . .

Make me believe, Make me laugh

Show me a sign, Give me a staff

Something of a bridge, a gift in my hour of need

Make it clever and broad

For my feelings to feed

Bring a smile to my face, never cease

To make me laugh.

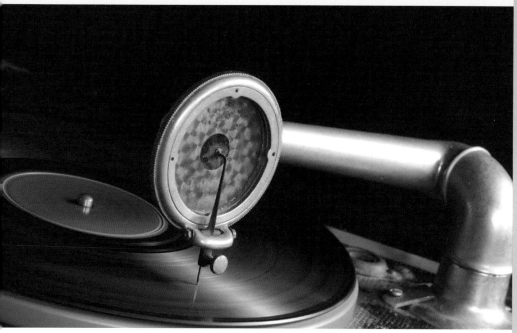

SOMEWHERE OVER THE RAINBOW

Y. HARBURG

Music by HAROLD ARLE

Freely, a cappella
Intro:
N.C.

When all the clouds dark-en up the sky-way, there's a rain-bow high-way to be

12

"Abstract Painting"
inspired by:

OVER THE RAINBOW
By: Judy Garland
Music: Harold Arien
Lyrics: E.Y. Harburg
Written for: "The Wizard of Oz"
Original Release Date: 1939
Genre: Ballad

13. Just Unique

9. I've never had to travel very far

7. It detects imperfection in my innermost song. I begin to cry

10. Music touches the innocence, my innocence

12. I am not so very deep that no other could contend

2. Unobserved and unabashed, where I am allowed to dance

3. There is a Bluebird on my shoulder and butterflies are free

8. As I am crying, love finds me close

5. I am smiling

11. Even snow plays a tune when falling, for those who choose to listen

4. The kingdom of sunshine has opened her arms to me

6. As I am smiling, an AWAC waltzes by

1. Somewhere among the clouds, just above Paris, France

Chapter 2

Fashioned by the Creator, Emboldened by my Maker

I've learned much and am ready to serve

Ready to receive the kind blessings that await me

That's found, in the spiritual roots of the Son.

"*Journey To The Day*"
inspired by:

Heaven is Ten Zillion Light Years Away
By: Stevie Wonder
Written by: Stevie Wonder
Album: "Fullfillingness' First Finale"
Original Release Date: 1974
Label: (Tamla) Motown
Genre: Soul, Funk

JOURNEY TO THE DAY

Why does my comfort level decline and fall
When I clasp my hands to pray
Why does my heart race, my mind slip
My eyes look away
Surely, I am not a non-believer
I believe with all of my heart
I trust in the winds and ways of our Father
Yet, praise Him in the dark

Journey to the day

When I am filled with Him
When I am resuscitated,
Rejuvenated by my alliance with Him
When my soul at rest, knows
When my taste for spiritual food is such
The hunger won't let me go

When I am altogether free of the tie that binds
And am on my way

To the day

To the day I find forgiveness, in the eyes of my Savior.

"To My Brothers of Mesopotamia"
inspired by:

Let It Be
By: The Beatles
Written by: Paul McCartney and John Lennon
Album: "Let It Be" (Beatles final album)
Original Release Date: 1970
Label: Apple Records
Genre: Rock, Pop, Gospel

TO MY BROTHERS OF MESOPOTAMIA

TO MY BROTHERS OF MESOPOTAMIA:

WE ARE ALL DESCENDANTS OF A GREATER GOD

DISCIPLES OF A GREATER GOOD

FROM THE TIMELESS WATERS OF THE EUPHRATES

TO THE SEQUOIAS OF REDWOODS

WE DESIRE WHAT IS NATURALLY OURS

BE IT IN HEAVEN OR HERE ON EARTH

LET NOT THE HAUNTING OF WAR DERAIL US

NOR THE LOGISTICS OF WHERE WE PRAY, DIVIDE US

WE WANT OUR OFFSPRING TO BE PROTECTED

OUR SOULS TO BE RESURRECTED

AND THE ASSURED EMBRACEABLE WARMTH

OF EVERLASTING LIFE

JOIN ME IN TEMPLE, IN MOSQUE, IN CHURCH, EN MASSE

THAT WE MAY BASK IN A UNITY UNBRIDLED AND HERETOFORE UNFED.

"I Thank God"
inspired by:

Oh Happy Day
By: Edwin Hawkins Singers
Written by: Edwin Hawkins
Album: "Let Us Go Into the House
    Of the Lord"
Original Release Date: 1968
Label: Pavilion/Buddah
Genre: Gospel

I Thank God

For every newborn baby in the arms of its mother

For every sounding Lark that stills the would-be passerby

For every sterling thought that leads to imagination

Every moment of tranquility, every mountain high

For every "whispering" eyes the artist wills to draw

For every stairway to happiness, every ladder to fame

For every Lilac smiling beneath Lady Sun

Every star turned on, every morning ablaze

I thank God

I thank God for the grandeur

And for the little things that mean so much.

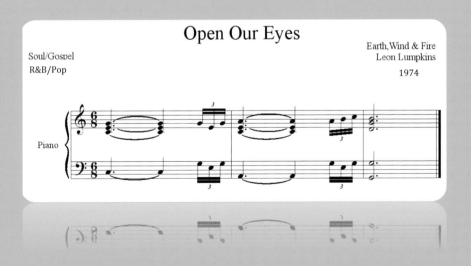

Open Our Eyes

Soul/Gospel
R&B/Pop

Earth, Wind & Fire
Leon Lumpkins
1974

Piano

"Sunday Morning Church Service"
inspired by:

Open Our Eyes
By: Earth, Wind & Fire
Written by: Leon Lumkins
Album: "Open Our Eyes"
Original Release Date: 1974
Label: Columbia Records
Genre: R&B, Pop

SUNDAY MORNING CHURCH SERVICE

It's Sunday morning

The music has stopped

And busy bodies are Alllllll up in my "secular" business

Using the "gifts" they say the Good Lord gave them

Like X-ray vision and mental telepathy

Leaning ears and Jealous eyes

Probing uninvited along my lonely pew

Feels like a drawn out, calculated game

Though quite possibly, I'm the only one playing

The lone entry in a surreal, paranoid round of "Chicken"

Absence woos a lady called Doubt

I've been away too long

I can't feel my legs

And Lord knows I'm a sinner

But it's Sunday morning

I'm praising my God

And ain't nobody perfect!

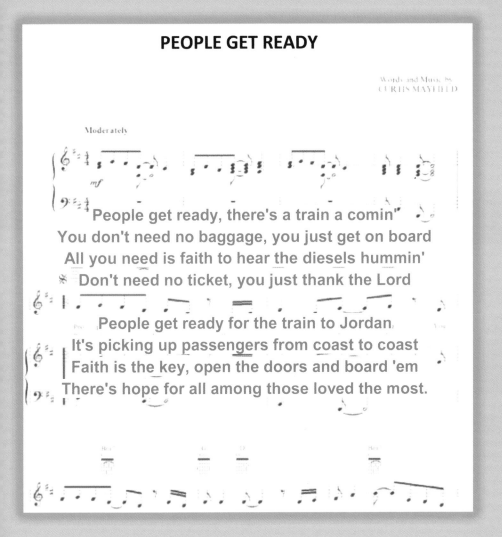

"On My Way"
inspired by:

People Get Ready
By: The Impressions
Written by: Curtis Mayfield
Album: "People Get Ready"
Original Release Date: 1965
Label: ABC - Paramount
Genre: Gospel, R&B

On My Way

God's glory has enveloped me this day

My body awash in glory by God

My feelings; untouched by the
fickle deeds of mortals

My spirit glides along an etched and
decorated wall

That bends at the last, upward

Symphony bells cascade, they ring
in unison

A conductor gestures and music
obediently begins to play

An angel alights from a cloud and
bids adieu

To the achingly beautiful and
conflicting lady

That is a distant planet earth

I rise along the wall and am ushered
forth into a new level of existence

Where age-old problems are remedied,
where my ancestors reside

To a place that is holy and undisturbed

By the wicked winds of judgment,
prejudice, echoes and lies

I am at peace

I do not crave for anything, for
anything sugary and sweet

For choice meats and specialty
fare to fill my belly

For alcohol to dull my senses

For slick clothing to represent me

whilst masking my nakedness

I can see, at once, an opening; an
expanding crevice in the atmosphere

At the mouth of which stands
someone familiar

Someone I've known for all of
my life, and yet,

I cannot offer a name, but all is well

As I don't believe it important
as the deed

This certain someone is leading me,
grooming me to a fare thee well

Ahhhh yes! A celebration!

I've been here before

Hello,

Again.

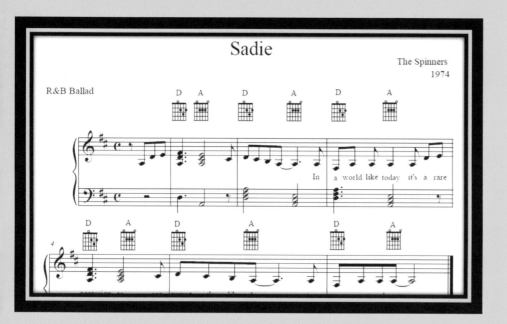

"Why I Believe"
inspired by:

Sadie
By: The Spinners
Written by: Bruce Hawes, Joseph
    Banks Jefferson, Brett
    Anderson, Charles B. Simmons,
    Richard Oakes.
Album: "New and Improved"
Original Release Date: 1974
Label: Atlantic
Genre: R&B

WHY I BELIEVE

Her body is frail, weathered from disease

Yet, she smiles, allegiance undeterred,

<u>It's Why I Believe</u>

She's counterpoint to hopelessness, A beacon of truth

The antithesis of cynicism, A stranger to youth

Yet, she presses on with uncanny youthfulness

Blessed with a contentment that belies her suffering

She is unsung

Yet, she is the most cherished woman in the world

We know her as the "Keeper of the Faith"

She instills in us lessons that bloom into wisdom

If we do her justice, we pay it forward

Encouraging one another to scale the good mountain

And when we arrive, we arrive with humility

With a humaneness that speaks in the vernacular of love

You may ask yourself; what power could engender such a spirit?

That of a Mighty Lord!

THE MISEDUCATION OF
LAURYN HILL

*"Let me be patient, let me be kind
Make me unselfish without being blind."*

**"Untitled
(the prayer)"**
inspired by:

Tell Him

By: Lauryn Hill
Written by: Lauryn Hill and
  Walter Afanasieff
Album: "The Miseducation of
  Lauryn Hill" (Solo Album)
Original Release Date: 1998
Label: Ruffhouse Records &
  Columbia Records
Genre: Neo-Soul

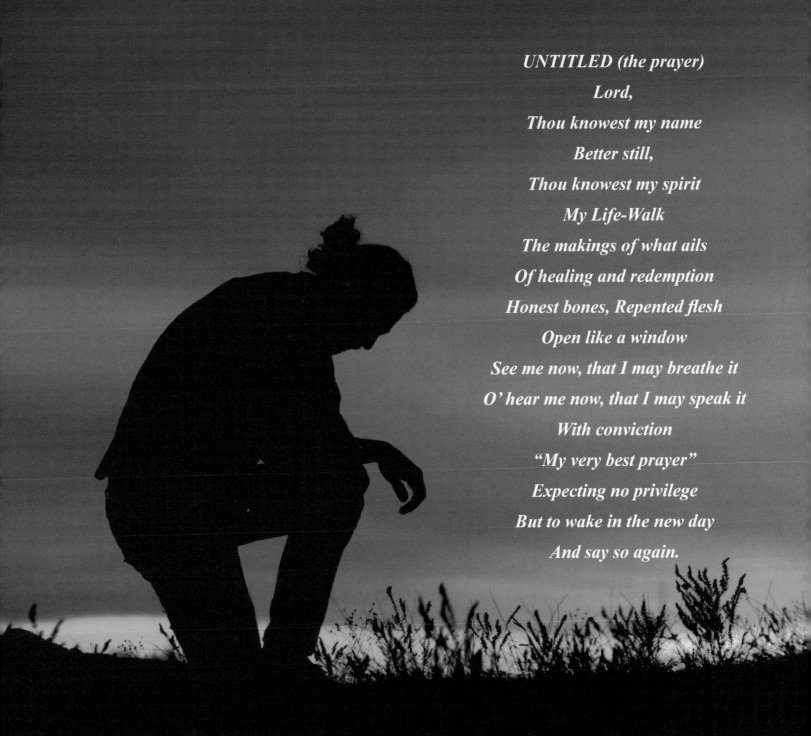

UNTITLED (the prayer)

Lord,
Thou knowest my name
Better still,
Thou knowest my spirit
My Life-Walk
The makings of what ails
Of healing and redemption
Honest bones, Repented flesh
Open like a window
See me now, that I may breathe it
O' hear me now, that I may speak it
With conviction
"My very best prayer"
Expecting no privilege
But to wake in the new day
And say so again.

Chapter 3

BLUE MOOD

From the valley of darkness, I rose to the light

Only to find my sunshine had found another place

Informed of an escapade in which she'd taken part

I'm ambivalent

about love

and its many masquerades.

"Twixt A Rock and a Hard Place"
inspired by:

I Want To Be Free

By: The Ohio Players
Written by: Willie Beck, Leroy
      Bonner, Marshall Jones,
      Ralph Middlebrooks,
      Marvin Pierce,
      Clarence Satchell,
      James L. Williams
Album: "Fire"
Original Release Date: 1974
Label: Mercury
Genre: Soul, Funk

TWIXT A ROCK AND A HARD PLACE

"Can't do wrong, Can't do right"
Holes in my interior, exposed overnight
Imperfections revealed to worlds' delight
I'm twixt a rock and a hard place

Bloody word-fare and false allegations
Wayward truths that shock the nation
My innards twist but I fail to speak
So as to calm the storm, keep the peace
Silent soldier, soldier to silence

I'm twixt a rock and a hard place

I'm trapped inside of a box
Surrounded by walls of contradiction
Love / hate the most haunting
Followed by doubt / conviction
While the voice of negativity screams
I dare not listen

I'm twixt a rock and a hard place

I do not believe in fate and destiny pre-determined
Nor in scripted, guaranteed light at the end of tunnels
My master plan evolves daily, I'm forever yearning
For happiness, sustenance, and the fruit of my labor
For my soulmate to emerge, for my eyes to grace her
Patient, but overdue,

I'm twixt a rock and a hard place.

I WISH IT WOULD RAIN

Words and Music by NORMAN WHITFIELD,
BARRETT STRONG and ROGER PENZABENE, SR.

"I Wish It Would Rain"
inspired by:

I Wish It Would Rain

By: The Temptations

Written by: Norman Whitfield,
Barrett Strong, & Roger
Penzabene

Album: "The Temptations - Wish
It Would Rain"

Original Release Date: 1967

Label: Motown (under the Gordy
imprint)

Genre: R&B

~ *I WISH IT WOULD RAIN* ~

That gorgeous September sky outside

Has not a clue about my feelings tonight

For if it truly understood the condition of the heart

And in particular, the incessant pain in mine

It would surely start to cry.

It would lower an angry brow, cast the cloudiest spell

Conjure up a wind, from "sea to shining sea"

It would seek to soothe my soul

While wreaking havoc from the heavens

As a sign of recognition and a show of empathy.

Tonight, I lie alone, in bed with but my thoughts

Blind to the reasons why, trying to find my way without

I've been fooled, duped by love

On a short sweet journey

To nowhere.

"Wisdom"
inspired by:

Nowhere Man

By: The Beatles
Written by: Lennon - McCartney
Album: "Rubber Soul"
Original Release Date: 1965
Label: Parlophone
Genre: Folk, Rock

Lord,

Where does one's wisdom lie?
Where does it nest?
Does it burrow so low that one can't see it?
Does it play a clever game of chance?
Is it borne of the heart? Or of the mind?
Is it destined to bloom? Or, dare I ask; can it be lost in time?

My inner compass will lead me to wisdom. I know it will
It'll wrest me from a sound sleep and demand my shoes put on
It'll rush me to the door, to the open air, and street
Where I will proclaim for all to hear; that I am at once, wise

But when, my Lord? When will I bear witness?
When will my palate lift, my voice command?
That I, myself, am a lion of a man
To be taken at his word, and indeed, his roar
A footnote to no one, an ambler nevermore

O Wisdom, where art thou?

37

"My Blue Epiphany"
inspired by:

Send in the Clowns

By: Glynis Johns - Frank Sinatra
    - Judy Collins
Written by: Stephen Sondheim
Written for: "A Little Night Music"
    Broadway Play
Original Release Date: 1973
Label: Reprise (on Frank Sinatra's
    album - "Ol' Blue Eyes is Back"
Genre: Ballad, later becoming both a
    Jazz standard and Pop song

MY BLUE EPIPHANY

When does it, where does it, and why does love go wrong?
Why does it come unglued, unhinged, unfastened, undone?

I believe we both came to reason;
that in the innocence of our youth
Were opportunities lost to taste forbidden fruit
Thus a mindset was borrowed, to re-capture
the grass green days
Fulfilling a lifelong ambition of fun and "Purple Haze"
Pour me deep, drink me slow
Read between my lines, my highs, my lows
This time, I offer everything there is to know
Of winters gone by and summers ago.

It was happenstance, as I recall, that I strayed
upon this flower
Dancing there, slowly, in the waning mid-night hour
Shapely, comely, a woman in the making
A budding superstar; I felt, mine for the taking
I pulled her close, and joined her in the dance
I was smitten, half-way down the aisle and bereft of chance
You see; one needs not a hint, one needs not a clue
When the lady of your life spins and smiles, at you
Oh how I loved her, loved her so
All those winters and summers ago.

Loved her like birds love their song in the morning
Like I love food, sunshine and Mother Earth
Making love in open "Fields of Gold"
Soul music in the club, gospel rhythms in church
The way a man ought to love, like good men do
Like Miles loved jazz and the lowdown dirty blues
She, my ultimate compliment, my truest power
My defining moment, my finest hour.

So when does it, where does it and why does
love go wrong?
Why does it come unglued, unhinged,
unfastened, undone?
And might it even matter, at the end of the day,
How the scales of justice lean and the
winds of hurt sway?

For I now know that I cannot fix love
Cannot scold it, reprimand it and demand
it come home
Can't command its attention if it's destined to roam
Realistically speaking, I've since learned
That is to say; I've come to conclude
That love will never revert back
Back to the lovely way that love used to be
So sad to report, my blue epiphany.

"SOMEONE SAVED MY LIFE TONIGHT"

Words and Music by
ELTON JOHN and BERNIE TAUPIN

"Sometimes You Just Wanna Quit"
inspired by:

Someone Saved My Life Tonight

By: Elton John
Written by: Elton John, Bernie Taupin
Album: "Captain Fantastic and the
    Brown Dirt Cowboy"
Original Release Date: 1975
Label: MCA (US/Canada)
    DJM Records
Genre: Soft Rock

SOMETIMES, YOU JUST WANNA QUIT

Sometimes, you just wanna quit
When the rainbow lets you know
It doesn't plan to show
Conveniently abandoning you
Just when you need it most.

Sometimes, you just wanna quit
Rambling voices about your head
Urgent business to be met
Life takes you for a flip
Makes you wanna quit.

Laughter is unbecoming
On this the gloomiest of days
Stormy weather comes to town
Thirty degrees in May.

Sometimes, you just wanna quit
And declare the merchandise sold
Passing the baton swiftly along
To some unsuspecting soul.

Tears In Heaven
featured in the Motion Picture RUSH

"Untitled"
inspired by:

Tears in Heaven
By: Eric Clapton
Written by: Eric Clapton,
    Will Jennings
Album: "RUSH" - initially featured in
    the Motion Picture "RUSH"
Original Release Date: 1992
Label: Warner Bros. Records
Genre: Soft Rock, Acoustic Blues

UNTITLED

You came into our world, asleep, without fanfare
Without the customary smiles in waiting
Without the triumphant sounds of trumpets,
    playing out sounds of joy
Without the pulsating beat of the drum,
    that was to be your heart
You took another route, yours was a darker fate
We never heard from you, for you were silent
We never came to know you,
    for you were gone before we knew
Time and circumstance forbade our family reunion.

You came into our world, a vision lost
Without pain, dependency, want or fear
You arrived unassuming and took nothing
Free you were, in the purest sense
You never cried, you never laughed
You took another path
Yours was a well-traveled but lonely path
Saturated by tears from those who wished you well.

Know that your father and mother love you
Know that for a moment, each would hold you close
To feel your soul
To whisper hello and kiss you goodbye
To confirm for history, and self, that you indeed had a place.

"Blue Sense"
(when a woman hurts)
inspired by:

When A Woman's Fed Up

By: R. Kelly
Written by: Robert S. Kelly
Album: "R"
Original Release Date: 1998
Label: Jive
Genre: R&B

BLUE SENSE
(when a woman hurts)

The BLUE see very well, very well indeed
Sight connected to heart, heart connected to mind
Tuned into each movement/transgression known to human kind
When you're hurt, truly hurting
 Things have a way of becoming acute

You can feel/*touch* everything, and then some
Taste the bitterness of the present, and the sweet nectar
     of the distant past
Can *smell* the roses that have long since withered at your feet
And the lingering scent from his imprint forged in your
     beautiful brass bed

There are no writing blockages of note, quite the contrary
Diaries are routinely filled the world over during these
     morose moments in time
Pain bespeaks verbalization, anger begets articulation
In prose, or the prettiest/damnedest poetry one has ever heard

Heard? You can *hear* everything, including his useless efforts
     to be silent
Creeping/crawling at all hours of the day/night
What a sound/sight!
You've been found hound, discovered/unearthed
Tried and convicted
By a jury of your played babes.

Photo Credit: Jupiterimages/Stock Photo/Photos.com

Chapter 4

Love Mood

A panoramic view of what winter

is about to do

We nestle together, you and I

And await the coming new.

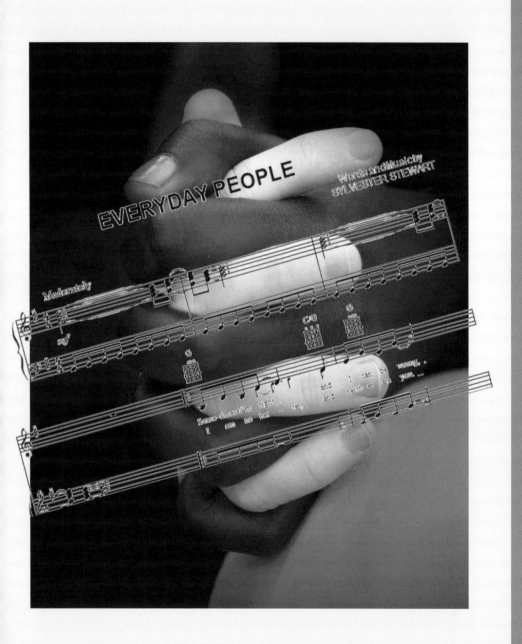

"A Friendship Found"
inspired by:

Everyday People
By: Sly and the Family Stone
Written by: Sylvester Stewart
Album: "Stand!"
Original Release Date: 1968
Label: Epic
Genre: Psychedelic Soul & Funk

A FRIENDSHIP FOUND

It was sheer caprice

A sudden attraction

An inadvertent brush of flesh

An involuntary reaction

You smiled at me

And barriers tumbled down

I smiled at you

And a friendship found.

"Love is Gonna Getcha"
inspired by

I'm Not in Love
By: 10 cc
Written by: Eric Stewart,
Graham Gouldman
Album: "The Original Soundtrack"
Original Release Date: 1975
Label: Mercury
Genre: Soft Rock

LOVE IS GONNA GETCHA

We often allow our hearts to lead us
Even when our mind knows best
Emotions build, peak, conquer
Leaving our soul a withering mess

Such is the way of love
The everyday play, ecstasy, and pain of love
Quiet and explosive, shallow and deep
Love is like the tide

We often pray for it, then fall prey to it
It can feed our ego or gnaw away at our insecurities
Forcing us to navigate in waters unexplored
Many lose their way, while others find the rainbow

Love can "F" you up or caress you gently
Trap you in its jaws or bathe you in glory
Write your plot, then change your story
Only "1" thing is certain,

LOVE IS GONNA GETCHA!

"The Dream"
inspired by:

**Just My Imagination
(Running Away With Me)**
By: The Temptations
Written by: Norman Whitfield,
Barrett Strong
Album: "Sky's the Limit"
Original Release Date: 1971
Label: Gordy
Genre: Psychedelic Soul

The Dream

A romantic novel opened wide at the base of your bed

Is yearning out loud for attention

Surrealistic images invented inside your head

Are dancing the dance of love

It is long after mid-night and the feeling is hot

A double fantasy of love is brewing

An erotic moon hovers while wind chimes sing

And awakening is you, with a need to be fulfilled.

You turn over slowly to gaze upon him at sleep

Steadfast in your conviction that he is subconsciously aware

His eyelids are heavy and his body is weak

He is about to encounter a dream and discover you there

He can feel lips pressing against a sensitive brow

He can see the dawn in a strange new light

The verdict on love will never be in question

As it is you at the helm of his dream, tonight.

Subconscious vibes are easily distorted

And a touch from you will bring about change

Various colors explode to excite his senses

The translation of each never the same

Difficult to decipher but his to enjoy

Are the kissing scenes with an unknown woman

Behind the scene and unbeknownst to him

You are at his chest and being woman.

Your man has his faults, as he is not perfect

He is at times, critical and impatient

But the one priceless gift you would never deny

Is the feeling he gave you when he described

The dream he'd had on that night of nights

The fun, the love, the spectacular lights

Two bodies clinging beneath sheets of lace

And how the unknown woman became familiar, in face

"It was you, my dear."

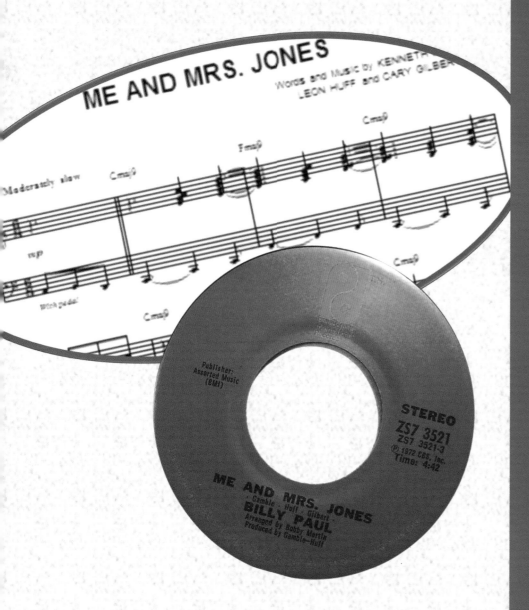

"A Love Forbidden"
inspired by:

Me and Mrs. Jones

By: Billy Paul

Written by: Kenny Gamble, Leon Huff,
Cary Gilbert

Album: "360 Degrees of Billy Paul"

Original Release Date: 1972

Label: Philadelphia International

Genre: R&B, Soul

~ A LOVE FORBIDDEN ~

I must admit, I am afraid

Afraid of getting too heavy

Compromised as we are

Hoping you'll be flattered

Praying that you'll smile, and look at me

Wishing I hadn't written, should a frown violate your face

But I guess it's a bit late.

I sometimes wonder if I love you / Especially when you're near

Earnest cravings, longings, all set to appear / Must once again seek refuge beneath the stoic mask

Brown eyes refulgent at the mere sight of you / Must tone down their glow and stray from the mark

An innocent victim of the heart, must continue to lie

I mustn't breathe, I mustn't reveal

I mustn't let on to the world how I feel

Intelligent, elegant female, succulent and fine / Silent movies and the art of pantomime

I am forbidden to speak, and wrong to dream

But wouldn't it be nice; if……..

"My Girl"
inspired by:

My Girl
By: The Temptations
Written by: William "Smokey"
    Robinson, Ronald White
Album: "The Temptations Sing
    Smokey"
Original Release Date: 1964
Label: Gordy (Motown)
Genre: Soul and R&B

MY GIRL

My Girl is Rich:

In the soil you know, the soul, inside and out, through and through.

My Girl is Spiritual:

Her alliance is with God, her faith everlasting.

My Girl is Unselfish:

A natural giver. She validates me in terms which are empowering and uplifting.

My Girl is Honest:

Righteous and pure. She listens in meaningful ways. The most trustful person I know.

My Girl is Family Oriented:

She takes care of her own. She plants seeds and cultivates them in her home.

My Girl is Passionate:

Fierce in her convictions, and beautifully and appropriately dramatic.

My Girl is Loyal:

Betray me not, leave me never.

My Girl is Forgiving:

She respects me for what I've become, and for what I strive to be.

My Girl Loves Me:

Amen!

Photo Credit: HyperionPixels/Stock Photo/Photos.com

"Our Love"
inspired by:

Our Love
By: Natalie Cole
Written by: Chuck Jackson,
Marvin Yancy
Album: "Thankful"
Original Release Date: 197
Label: Capital
Genre: Soul

OUR LOVE

The language of love has inspired me to speak

To lift my innermost feelings from confining walls of heart

And gently carry them to surface.

"When I've had enough of this and my mind is filled with that

When the world seems to rest upon my weary shoulders

It's good to be in love

When I brush your face in the middle of the night

When I warm you plenty and bring you to flight

Chase droplets from your body, and lick them with delight

I feel the pleasures of love

I feel a sense of unity, re-discovering you in the rawest of ways

Collaborative sounds of confirmation echoing from within

Revealing riffs, moans that tell and feline like purrs

Hallelujah!

I've someone, who fills my life to brim."

PRETTY WINGS

Words and Music by
MUSZE and HOD DAVID

"Confession"
inspired by:

Pretty Wings

By: Maxwell
Written by: Maxwell, Hod David
Album: "BLACKsummers'night"
Original Release Date: 2009
Label: Columbia
Genre: R&B, Neo-Soul

Confession

I raised the roof and chased the cat

Brushed aside feelings that in the end, mattered most

Alienated and shredded every fiber of love

While ego tripping along the corridors of bachelorhood

That was my way; I kept my feelings at bay, and

sacrificed my good spirit

For the victory: The short term promise of acute

gratification

For the conquest: The nightly escapades that rendered

me famous (infamous)

And while I believed myself content

It was all a figment of my singular, unhitched

imagination

However daunting, the truth of the matter is;

I only ever found love, when love inexplicably found me

Now I know the value of, the true value, of reciprocity

I love my woman! For all of the beautiful reasons,

And more.

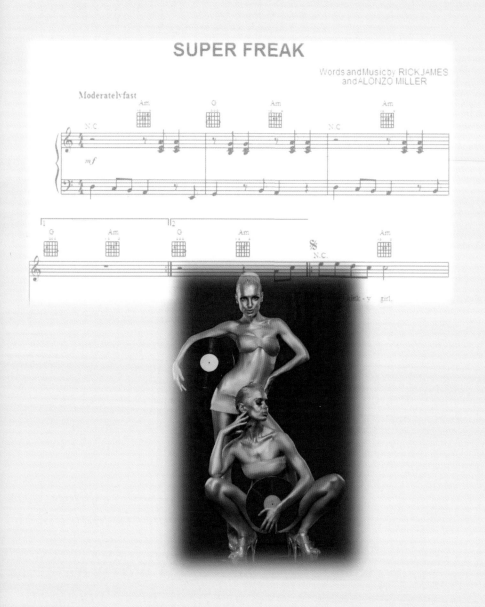

"Damn! Baby!"
inspired by:

Super Freak

By: Rick James
Written by: Rick James, Alonzo Miller
Album: "Street Songs"
Original Release Date: 1981
Label: Gordy
Genre: R&B, Funk

Damn! Baby!

I've got a sweet ache in my heart,
I don't have the words

I've been climbed by the mountain,
the oceans have surged

Consequently, I don't have the strength, the
wind, or the nerve

Can't say I saw this coming,
as I can be a tad bit controlling

Mind bound and utterly Ravished,
by a tigress in lamb's clothing

I knew my honey had tricks,
But DAMN! BABY!

63

YOU'RE SO VAIN

Words and Music by
CARLY SIMON

"The Fisherman"
inspired by:

You're So Vain
By: Carly Simon
Written by: Carly Simon
Album: "No Secrets"
Original Release Date: 1972
Label: Elektra
Genre: Soft Rock & Adult
     Contemporary

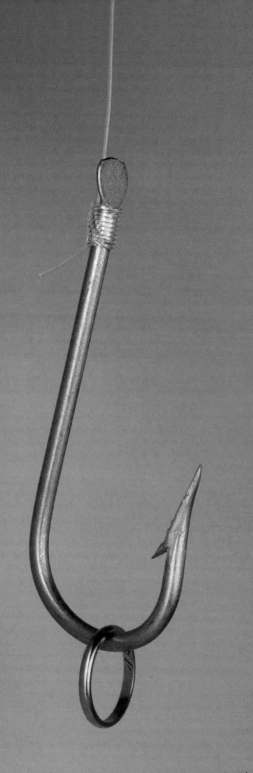

THE FISHERMAN

He'll compliment you endlessly with reassuring line

He'll butter you up in finger licking broth

Baiting patiently with wide scale experience

The fisherman lies in strategic wait

He cleverly schemes on a school of prey

Closing the distance of the costly strike

Selfishly envisioning the falling in love

A chance to use, the instant you BITE!

Chapter 5

I saw journeymen drunkards babble in sleep

I saw dreams of gold vanish at the awakening

I saw death as a novelty, beneath my window

Deep in the bowels of a disrespected land

Where dusk had long since arrived.

FIGHT THE POWER

from *DO THE RIGHT THING*

Words and Music by ERIC SADLER,
KEITH BOXLEY, JAMES BOXLEY III and CARLTON RIDENHOUR

Moderate (♫ = ♩ ♩)

C9 G♭13 F13 A♭9 sus G9 sus C7(♭9)

N.C.

Dou - ble - U   E.   L.   O.   V. ___ E. ___   F.   M. ___

(Spoken:) One, oh, eight

"Education Reparation"
inspired by:

Fight the Power
By: Public Enemy
Written by: Carlton Ridenhour,
              Eric Sadler,
              Hank Boxley,
              Keith Boxley
Album: "Fear of a Black Planet"
Original Release Date: 1989
Label: Motown
Genre: Political Hip Hop

It's so taboo as to be unspeakable in most circles of American Life
Offensive altogether to many blacks, and most of those white
And so we've kept silent, kept it chained in our guilt laden throats
Leery of reprisal, ridicule and shame

Dare I say it? Come on now . . . The REPARATIONS word

Seems to some absurd,
Conniving, unseemly, like some sick, wannabe verb
Fraudulent and undeserving of the time it takes to mouth it
But upon closer examination, it's clear our blatant procrastination
Ought to be written about, screamed about, and discussed calmly

This is not about blame, but it is about healing
Healing and patching a divide that leaves in its wake
Open wounds and psychological despair
And while we as a people continue to prosper and persevere
We are leaving a glaring work undone

Education should be free for us,
In recognition, as reparations for us

For the descendants of those forced to endure the brutal hardships
Of the Middle Passage.

EDUCATION REPARATION

FLAMENCO SKETCHES

By MILES DAVIS

"The Still"
inspired by:

Flamenco Sketches
By: Miles Davis
Written by: Miles Davis, Bill Evans
Album: "Kind of Blue"
Original Release Date: 1959
Label: Columbia
Genre: Jazz

THE STILL

Nocturnal creatures converging, congregating outside my window
Rippling through the trash, creeping in the shadows
Unmoved and unswayed, their presence alarms me not
For I tonight am silent, unyielding,
And distraction needn't try during the reigning of the Still.

I have often heard the older folk say;
"To warrant such a peace, one subject must lay in celestial preparation."
I must disagree, for residing in me now is grand serenity
I can feel a vibrant heart; I can draw a tear, and may
A human instrument begins to play
Through privileged brown eyes, a tear rushes to trickle
Sentimental parts of me are blooming in the Still
Like the sculptor awakening the dry sleeping stone
I am a poet feeling a need to convey
Knowing all too well
At some convenient moment during the darkness
Through relenting pores or secret doors
It will escape
Leaving the mind somewhat confused and the soul ajar
I must sing!
For such is the Still, it may never return.

"After the Storm"
inspired by:

Fragile
By: Sting
Written by: Sting
Album: "Nothing Like the Sun"
Original Release Date: 1988
Label: A&M
Genre: Acoustic Rock

AFTER THE STORM

It often takes the storm, deadly and dark
To induce a new beginning or family reunion
When tragedy is upon us and sadness looms
Our eyes search for deliverance, our hearts, for love.

Pass the cup my newfound friend / And let us both drink from the well

Although our differences are many, and steep / With class structure and the like, the poor and the elite

You ignored me / While I assured you that our lives would never touch

Now we embrace, we even commit / For the coldness of grief has brought ourselves here

Under one roof to shiver and mourn.

But after the storm, ahhhh, when all is quite calm / When our thundering woes have quieted and healed

When yesterday's tears have dried / When certainty again runs rampant in our lives

Will we continue in earnest to share the common well?

So much we have learned in this eerie weather / Till clouds form again are we destined to wait?

Convincing ourselves that love is second rate.

After the storm comes sun and test / Springtime summons the highest bidder

Will we walk forward or settle for less? / Ways of old our constant sitter

After the storm the trumpet will blow / After the storm, we will truly know

If our love is alive, pure and clean / Or merely selfish, opportunistic, fragmented, and lean.

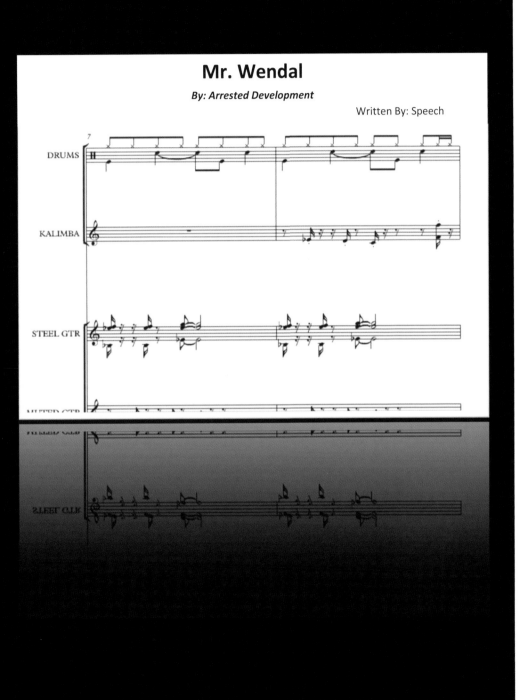

"A Friendship Found (2)"
inspired by:

Mr. Wendal

By: Arrested Development
Written by: Speech
Album: "3 Years, 5 Months and 2 Days in the Life Of..."
Original Release Date: 1992
Label: EMI/Chrysalis Records
Genre: Alternative Hip Hop, R&B

A FRIENDSHIP FOUND

A homeless old man sat frozen,
On a bench.
Unable to break his gaze,
Which was firmly fixed,
On his plight.
The rays of August failed,
To warm him.
The threat of eviction failed,
To move him.
His heart was heavy,
His options few.
As a steady stream of faceless people,
Hurried past.
The old man grew weaker,
In faith.

Just then,
He raised his head,
And allowed himself to see.
He looked forward,
And saw abstract pictures of death,
And despair.
He looked left,
And saw children frolicking,
In an endless sea,
Of pain.

He looked right,
And saw sitting next to him,
At his feet,
An old, lonely looking,
And perhaps homeless,
Crossbreed of a dog,
With an endearing face,
And an understanding disposition.

They sat quietly,
Apparently,
As they had been for some time.
Finally,
The old man lifted himself up,
To leave.
The dog followed,
And off they went,
Into the August sun,
That had previously failed,
To warm him.

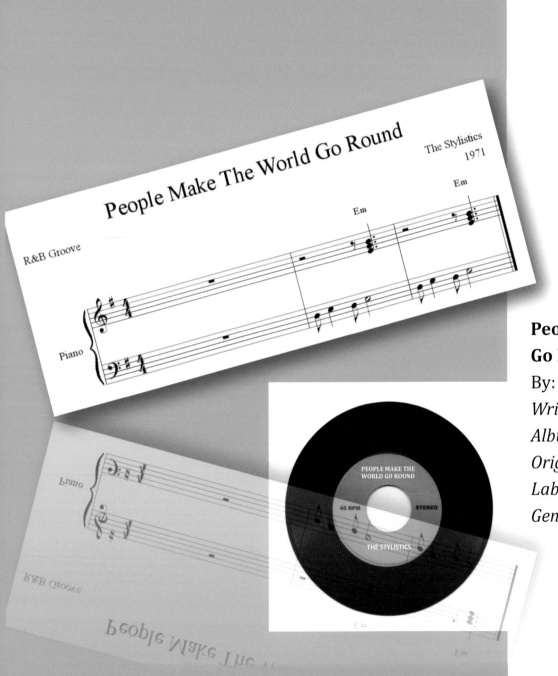

"The Underdog"
inspired by:

**People Make the World
Go Round**
By: The Stylistics
Written by: Thom Bell, Linda Creed
Album: "The Original Debut Album"
Original Release Date: 1971
Label: Avco/H&L
Genre: Soul, R&B

THE UNDERDOG

The minutes are painfully dissipating as you struggle to take hold

You are now mid-way through this grueling race

Around the bend, the burning stretch screams out in desperation

For an all-out rescue

For you to have a miracle finish by letting slip the weight

While others openly mock, belittle your very stride

You manage to remain proud, ever churning, unwavering

This great long run.

"Catch me if you dare," taunts the favorite in the lead

To the heavy breathing underdog, frazzled and out of steam

Sputtering in the wind, you are easily left behind

And all is not fair in the game of life.

"Stand"
inspired by:

**Say It Loud – I'm Black
And I'm Proud**
By: James Brown
Written by: James Brown
Album: "A Soulful Christmas and
Say It Loud – I'm Black and
I'm Proud"
Original Release Date: 1968
Label: King
Genre: Funk

S T A N D

A grieving Mother Africa speaks to her children

To her sons and daughters torn from her breast

Coerced into conforming to lifetimes of degradation

Forced to forget their lineage, their heritage, their culture

The wondrous history that makes the black one proud

Her children were contaminated with untruths

Blinded by systematic schools of darkness

Still recovering from conditions so cold and tragedies so terrific

That world wars pale in comparison

Mother Africa feels in her heart that the time is right

Her children have learned, are seasoned and bright

Ready-made warriors seeking truth that only dignity, pride and self-awareness can deliver

Mother Africa speaks to the African American:

Stand! If you have ever dueled against the mighty ministers of racism

Stand! If you absorbed their blows and forged forward with fortitude and grace

If you feel for your fathers and mothers who slaved in the field

With sweat on their brow and blood on their back,

Then stand, for your family

And prepare your offspring to reap the riches of the sun

Be wonderful and unwavering

Like a sculpture made of rock

Like a mountain topped in glory

Like a champion, poised and stout

Never lie down,

S T A N D

It's like a jungle sometimes it makes me wonder
How I keep from going under
It's like a jungle sometimes it makes me wonder
How I keep from going under

"Tellin' It"
inspired by:

The Message
By: Grandmaster Flash and the
  Furious Five
Written by: Ed "Duke Bootee"
  Fletcher, Grandmaster
  Melle Mel,
  Sylvia Robinson
Album: "The Message"
Original Release Date: 1982
Label: Sugar Hill
Genre: Old School Hip Hop,
Political Hip Hop, Electro

TELLIN' IT

Hunger passes my throat and down

Pain invades my belly, Anger fills my head

Sounds of sorrow reverberate but I cannot hear

Too focused on my wishes of honey and bread.

"Triumph"
inspired by:

What's Going On
By: Marvin Gaye
Written by: Al Cleveland,
    Marvin Gaye, Renaldo "Obie"
    Benson
Album: "What's Going On"
Original Release Date: 1971
Label: Tamia
Genre: Soul, R&B

TRIUMPH!

EXPRESS YOURSELF!
BE YOURSELF!
OPEN YOUR MIND!
KNOW YOURSELF!
WAKE FROM YOUR SLEEP!
CARRY THE TORCH!
TEACH YOUR CHILDREN!
PASS THE BATON!
SO THEY MAY LEARN!
THE WAYS OF THE WORLD!
AND TEACH THEIR CHILDREN!
TO STAY AWAKE!
TO OPEN THEIR MINDS!
TO HELP THEIR PEOPLE!
TO BE THEMSELVES!
AND WIN THE RACE!

Chapter 6

FAMILY MOOD

When but four, my grin in the sun did shine

While a lovely front yard bore the colors of the time

I remember quite vividly the moment fine

When grandma came to call.

"My Son"
inspired by:

Beautiful Boy (Darling Boy)
By: John Lennon
Written by: John Lennon
Album: "Double Fantasy"
Original Release Date: 1981
Label: Geffen Records
Genre: Pop Rock

"Life is what happens to you while you're busy making other plans."

MY SON

People say that you
remind them of me

That your look and demeanor
are owed to pedigree

Although I'm proud
and love this life that came to be

Your life's path is your own.

CAN'T TAKE MY EYES OFF OF YOU

Words and Music by BOB CREWE and BOB GAUDIO

Moderately

You're just too

good to be true, ____   can't take my eyes off of you. ____   You'd be like

LAURYN HILL

"Can't Take My Eyes Off Of You" - 1998

"Look at Her"
inspired by:

Can't Take My Eyes Off Of You
By: Frankie Valli
Written by: Bob Crewe, Bob Gaudio
Album: "The 4 Seasons Present
    Frankie Valli Solo"
Original Release Date: 1967
Label: Phillips Records
Genre: Pop Rock

Look at her

Look at that skin

Dark, beaming and
beautiful

The lady is a panther

A coal colored cat

A black lioness in sexy
green grass

She moves at once with
elegance and grace

Communicating,
stimulating and always
alluring

The theft of your heart,
your breath whisked away

And without a hint of rude
behavior

She conquers your soul.

Look at her

Look at this child

She was born gorgeous

Pristine, black and wonderful

Nothing less than a brilliant star

She is a wind song

A breezy melody on a quiet afternoon

When she smiles, her rays go straight to the heart

When she cries, it is all the more reason to love her

Nubian princess poised to take your throne

Sleep my dear and let your dreams carry you home.

Look at her

Look at her resolve

The thrill is in no way gone

She leaves you with a

thought to ponder

A prayer on Sunday morn

Tell us a story grandma, one

ditty for the living

One proud remembrance

from an esteemed life of

giving

You were the one, you kept

us strong

Guardian of the light,

religion and song

Owing you, knowing you,

loving you, black woman.

Look At Her

"Golden Lady"
inspired by:

Golden Lady
By: Stevie Wonder
Written by: Stevie Wonder
Album: "Innervision"
Original Release Date: 1973
Label: Motown
Genre: Soul

You're such a helpful lady

A golden lady

A passion filled, grand and genuine, kind of lady

An endearing, honest and fair lady

As quick to praise a stranger, as you would a lifelong friend

You're a respectful lady

A thankful lady

A child rearing, God fearing, spiritual kind of lady

Kindness of heart

Blessed from the start

Your days will be remembered, and your ways revered

You're an impact lady

An assertive lady

A trailblazing, pioneering, groundbreaking kind of lady

A galvanizing, energizing and persistent lady

Destined to succeed and determined to make a difference

You're a freedom fighter lady

A civil rights lady

One of the first to wear your hair short and natural,
   kind of lady

A frontline lady

A grassroots lady

Steady as steel

Ready and real

And miles ahead of your time

You're an educated lady

An intelligent lady

A smart, eloquent, and learned lady

A teaching, tutoring, and nurturing kind of lady

Ever willing to lend an ear, or when needed, a word

You're an unsung lady

A patient lady

A spectacularly modest and humble kind of lady

True to your convictions

Enriching and uplifting

All of whom came your way

Such a captivating lady

An autumn lady

A colorful, cool and wholesome kind of lady

Ever regal, always the consummate lady

Gorgeous in your day

Though aging and gray

Your beauty remains now and new

And so you are, that rarest lady

The kind that gives more than she receives, daily

An honorable, upright and righteous lady

Never discriminating

Always illuminating

And, golden.

G O L D E N   L A D Y

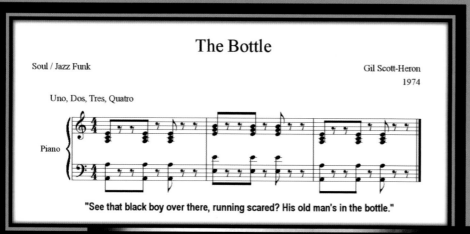

The Bottle

Soul / Jazz Funk

Gil Scott-Heron
1974

Uno, Dos, Tres, Quatro

Piano

"See that black boy over there, running scared? His old man's in the bottle."

"Just Like Em"
inspired by:

The Bottle
By: Gil Scott Heron & Brian Jackson
Written by: Gil Scott Heron
Album: Winter in America
Original Release Date: 1974
Label: Strata-East
Genre: Soul, Jazz-Funk

JUST LIKE EM

The resemblance is uncanny,
but I knew him not

I've seen his photograph
paired next to mine

Fearful the similarities will
continue to mount

My daddy's in the mirror, in
my eyes.

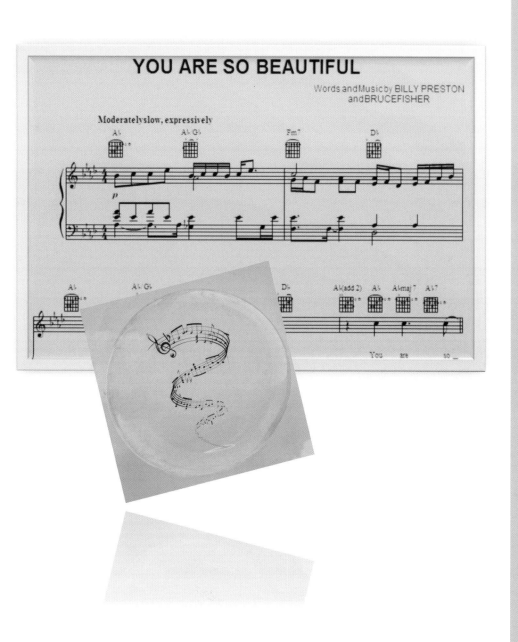

"Think of One"
inspired by:

You Are So Beautiful
By: Joe Cocker
Written by: Dennis Wilson,
    Billy Preston, Bruce Fisher
Album:" I Can Stand a Little Rain"
Original Release Date: 1974
Label: A&M
Genre: Pop, Blue Eyed Soul

Think of One

One love has spawned a diamond
So beautiful to life
Quiet sleeps our cornerstone
Flawless in the night
She awakes in morning to say;
"How I love the both of you."

And there is indeed radiance
In her smile from the heart
Soft eyes conducting
Commanding my arms
To hurry and hold

And I'll betcha she dreams
In fudge brown color
Butterscotch sweet
With more left over
My darling is a lot like rain

For a taste of brand new
I am constantly allowed
Each and every time
She comes down
Love flowing in me now
As I think of one.

Chapter 7

The finest of gifts may linger in a soul

Parade in its midst and never be found

But when thoroughly searched for

With the light of inspiration

The wails of defeat rarely sound.

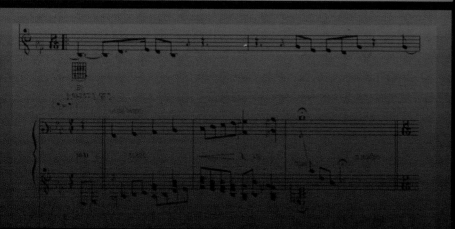

Rap
"Chicago on Fire!"
inspired by:

A Change is Gonna Come
By: Sam Cooke
Written by: Sam Cooke
Album: "Ain't That Good News"
Original Release Date: 1964
Label: RCA Victor
Genre: Soul, R&B

CHICAGO ON FIRE!

Bloody tourniquet wound tight, baby brother's still breathing
His sister clenches, pinches, presses, prays for healing
She's alone, afraid, underage but unyielding
"A day in the life", Just another day in the life.

Babies gettin' shot up! It's happening on our watch!
Don't look at your stop watch! Cause watchin' it won't stop it!
Sister's shouts screaming out! Baby Brother's bleeding out!
Retribution revolution, stray shots bound to choke him out.

Everybody's blood's up! The hood's a pressure cooker
Teeming Turmoil in a pot, the sight will make u sicker
"Bloody Sundays", Mondays, rivers, drops and stains
The reaper calls, the parlor makes good, everybody pays.

Territorial footprints, markers on the block
Cannibalism, color wars, all black on black
Burning flesh, heated fresh, the fire from the barrel
Smoking guns, Rivals run, they'll never see tomorrow.

Chicago on Fire, generations past dire
Imploding, exploding, a race to get higher
Hurricanes in alleys, flipping cars, popping molly
Niggas stormin', terror's the norm;
Murder's the new Bob Marley, "1 Love?"

Black boys get arrested, locked up and tested
Many lose, get fooled, tried and bested
And when they get out, it's back to the grind
Un-rehabilitated, on the same corner they left behind
It's cyclical, predictable, matter over mind
"A Change is Gonna Come", but we're generations behind.
Dreams unfulfilled, We take more than we give
We choose death over life, We die before we live
Evening news come & gone, nothing new, nothing's wrong
A Bloody tourniquet cast aside, Baby Brother's gone.